Wicked Saphic Erotica

exotic adult coloring

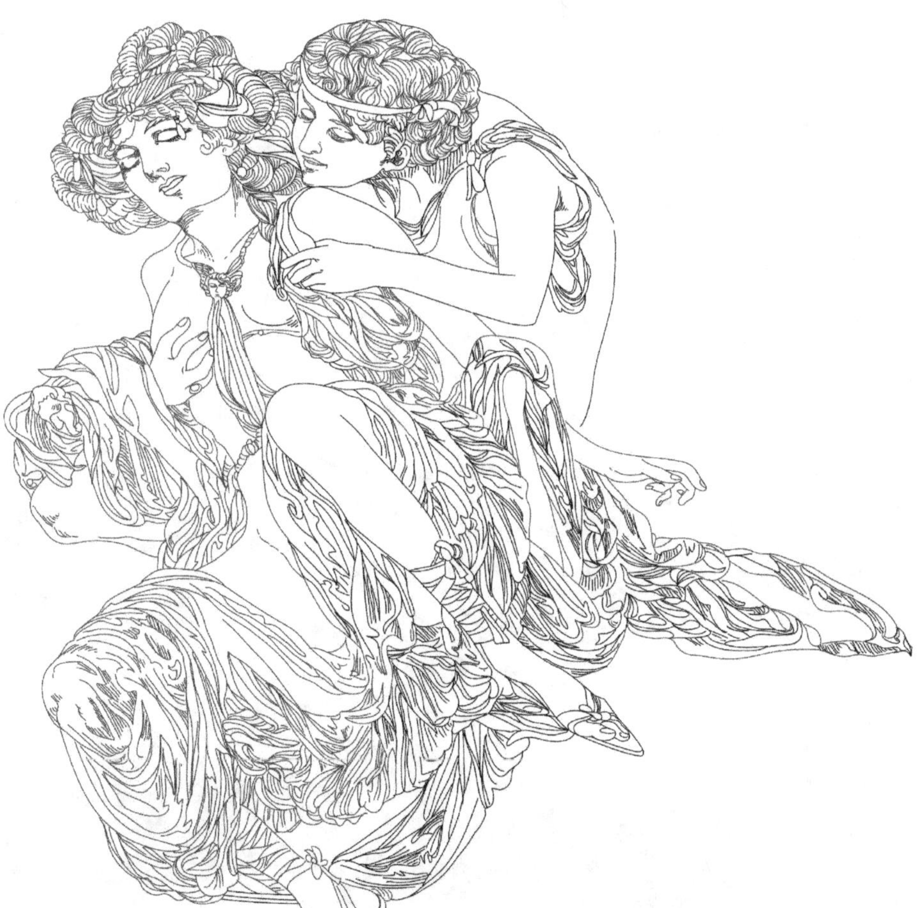

by Natalie Tate

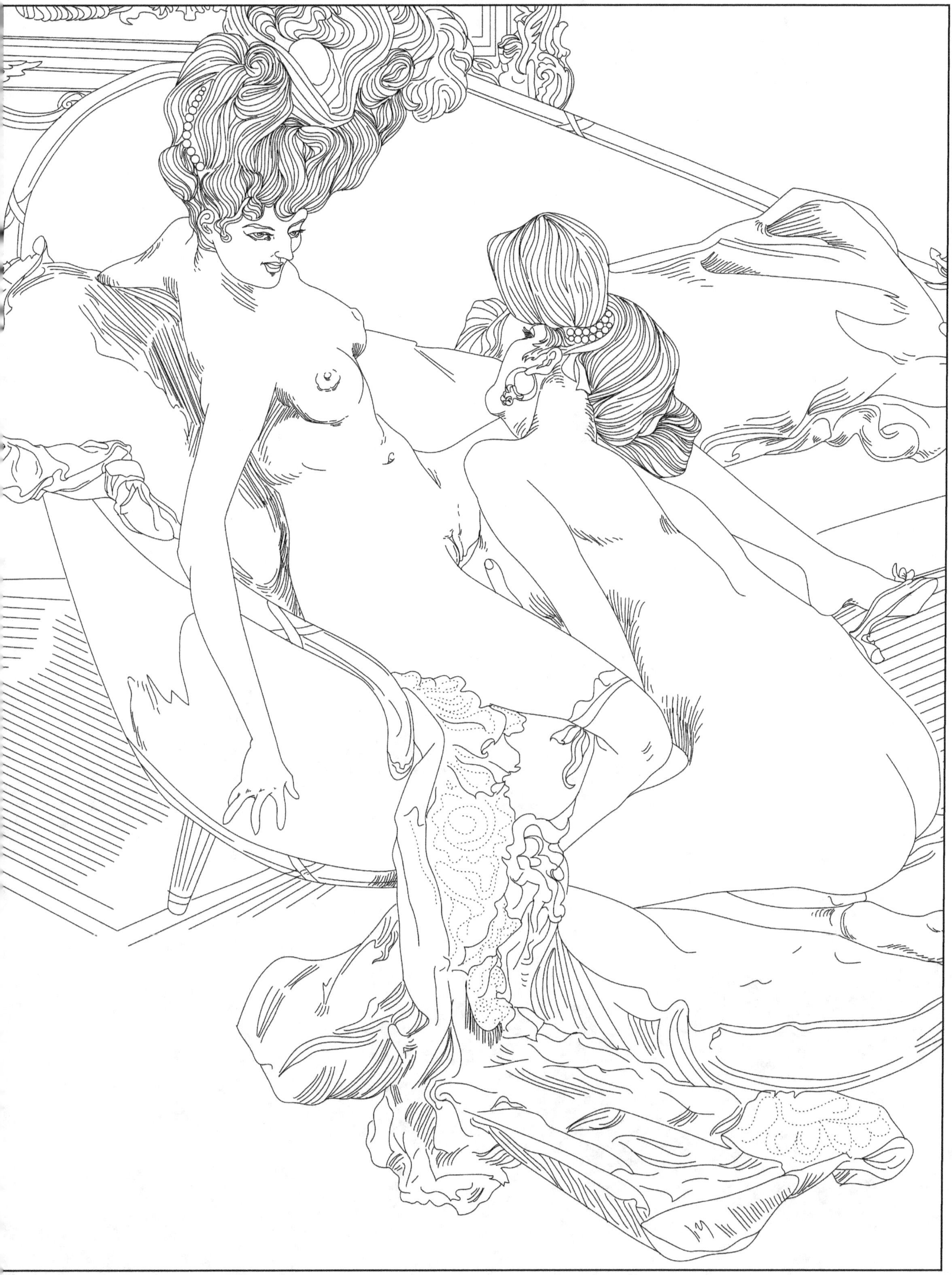

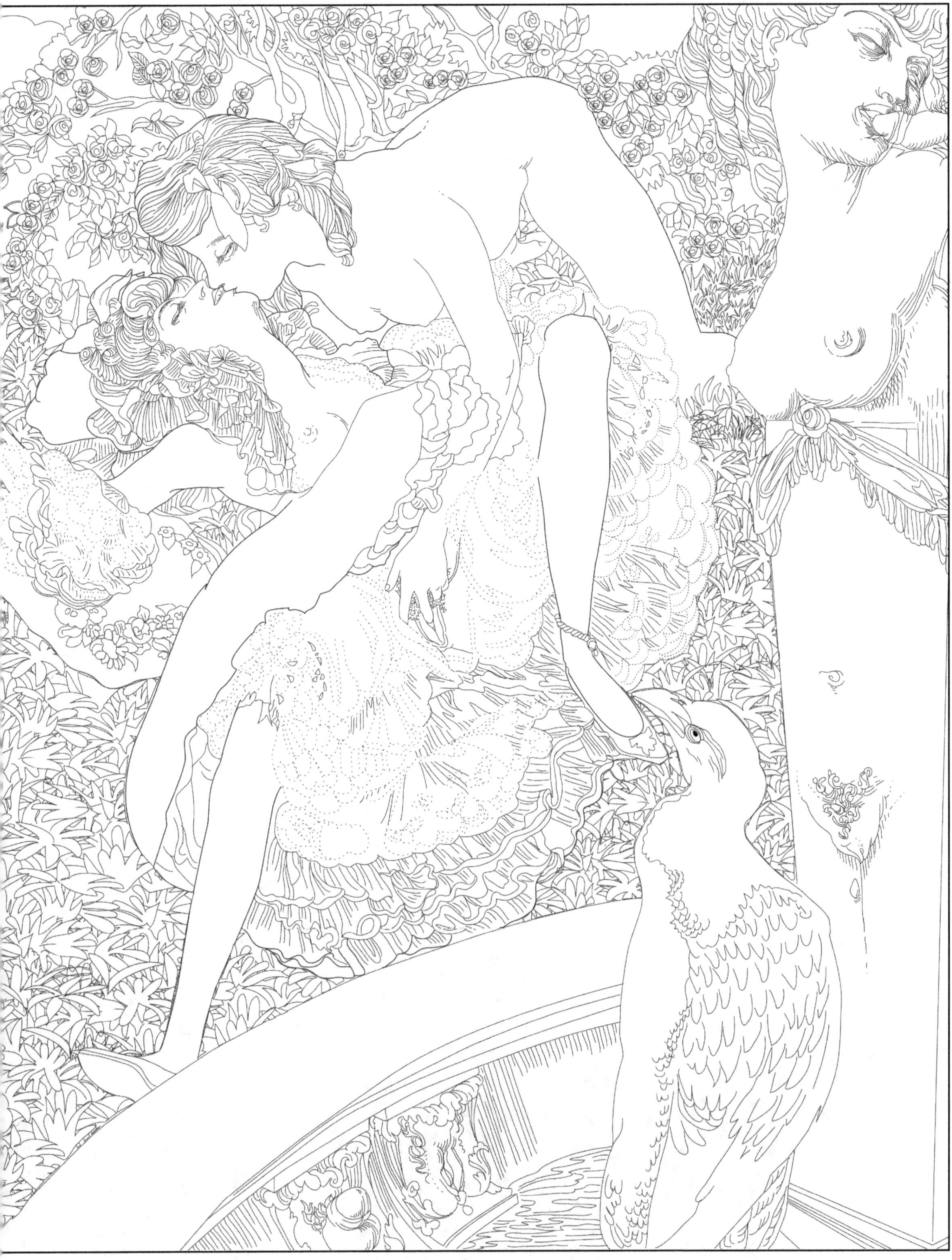

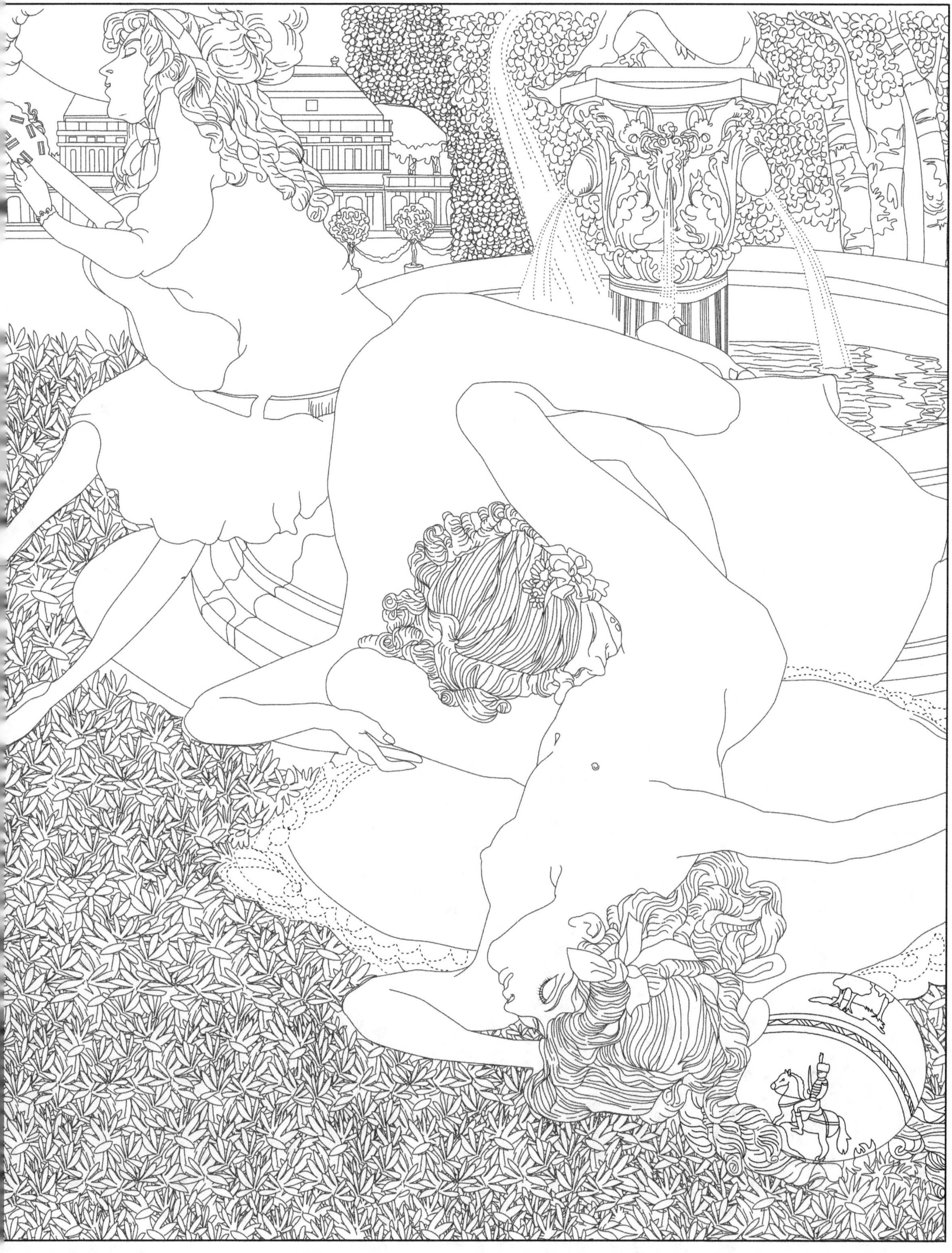

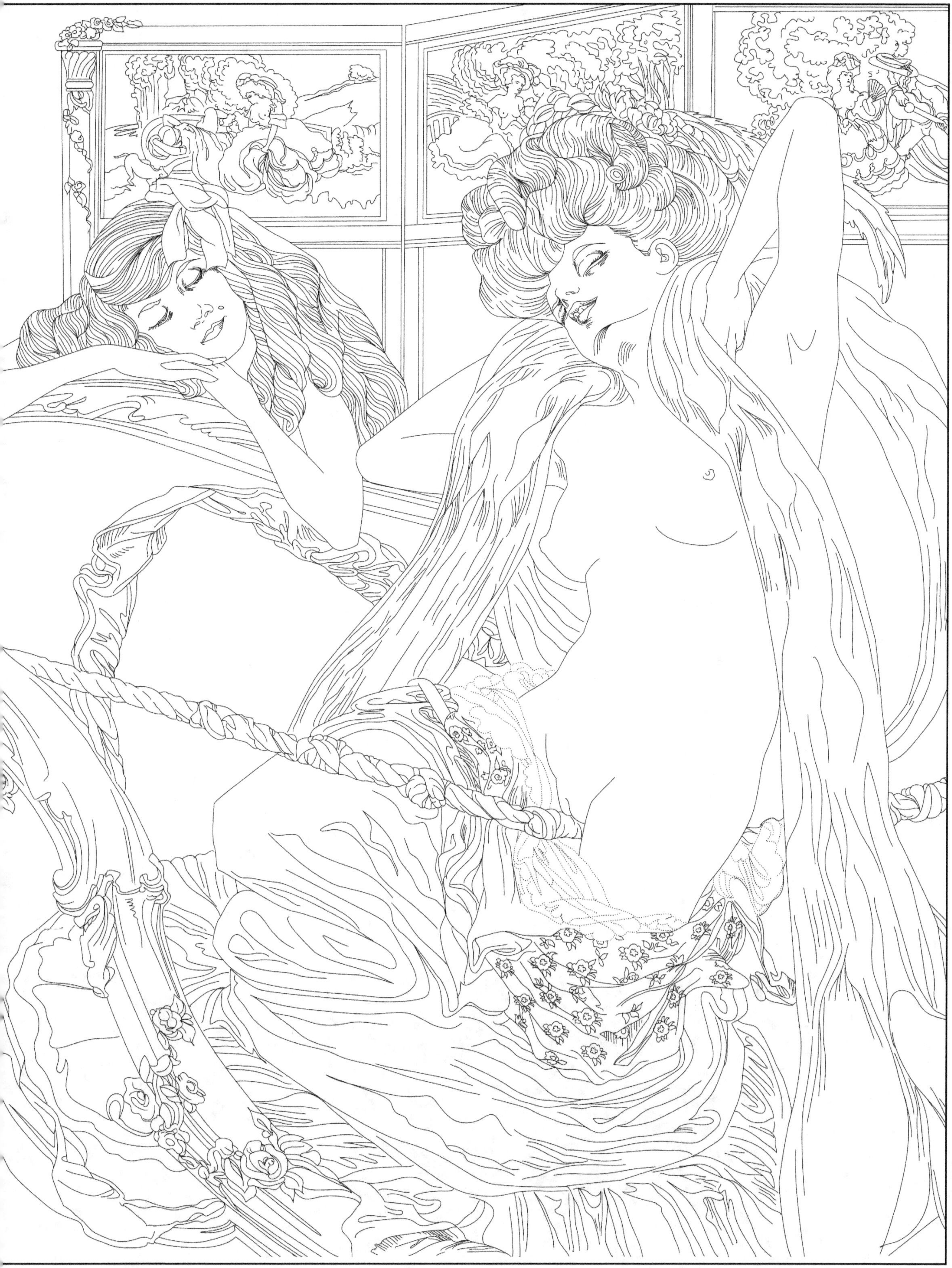

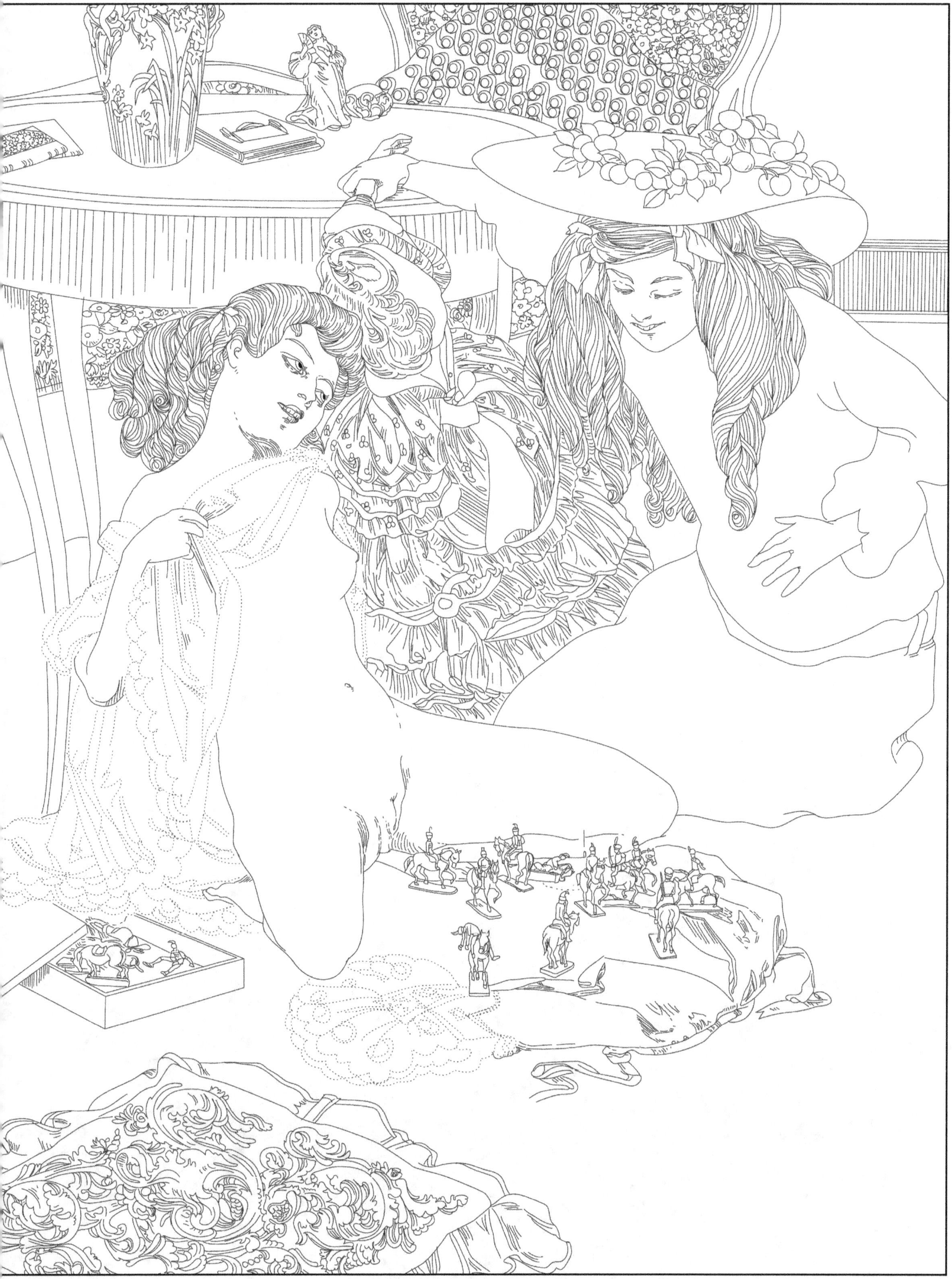

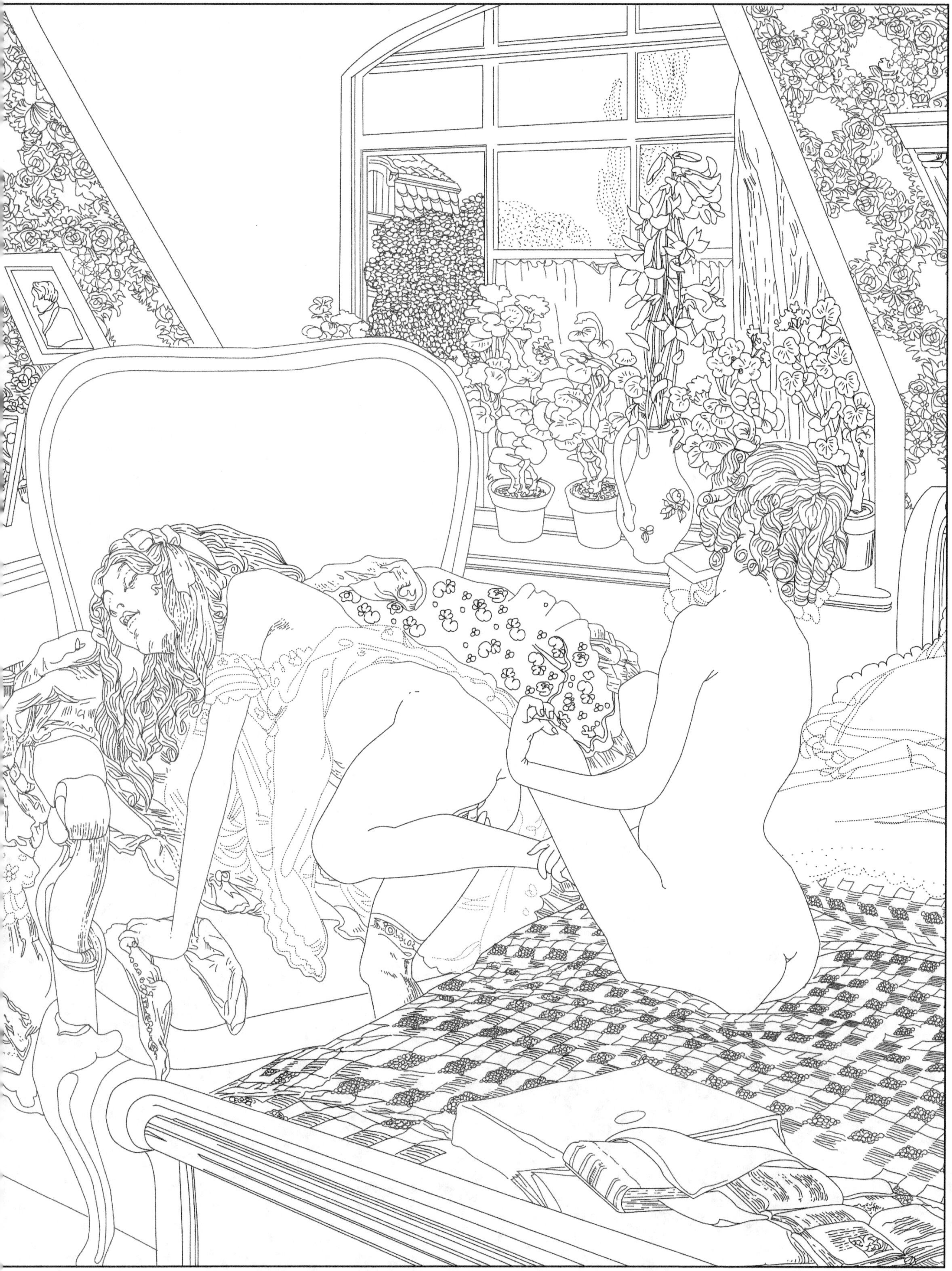

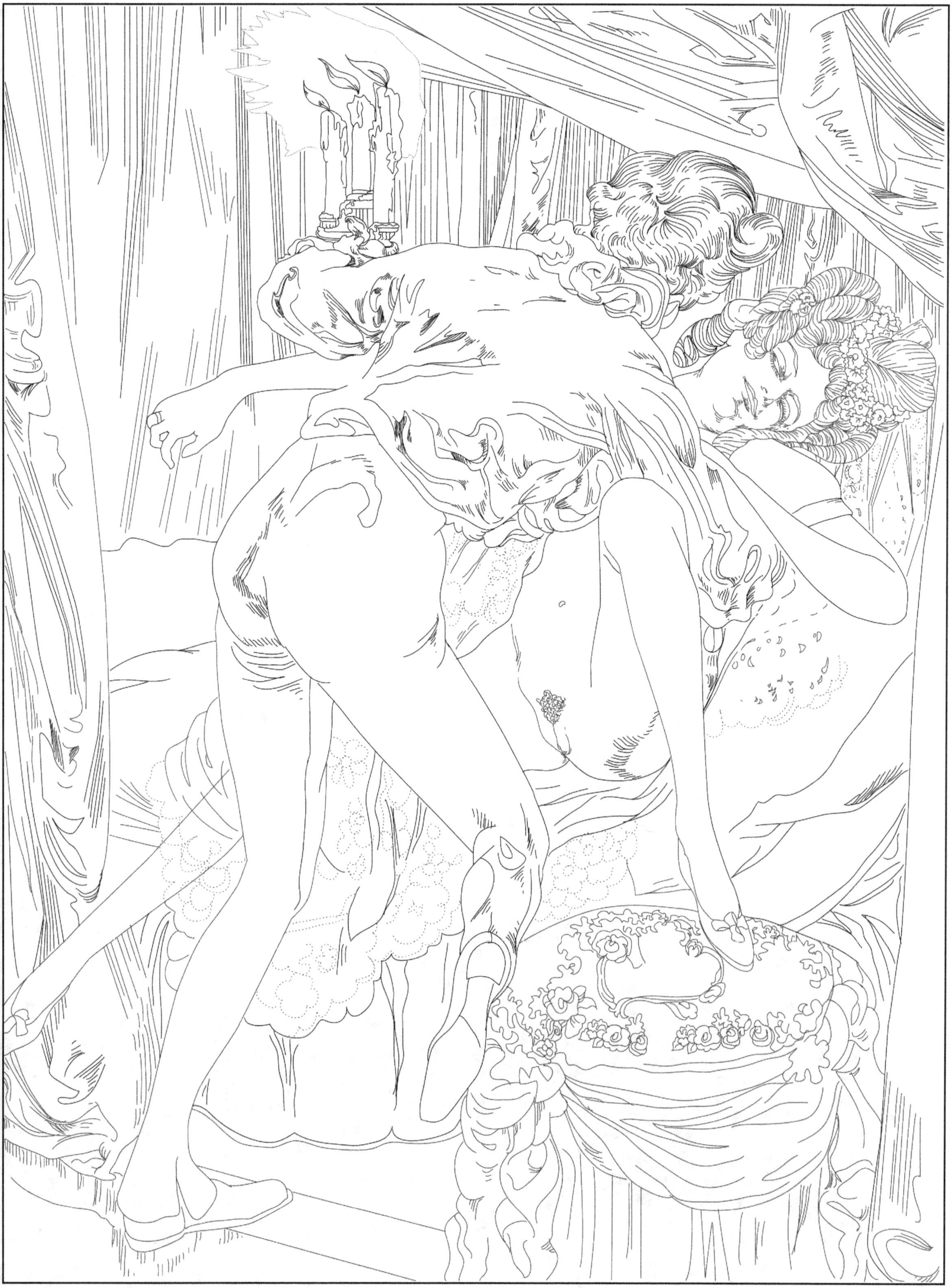

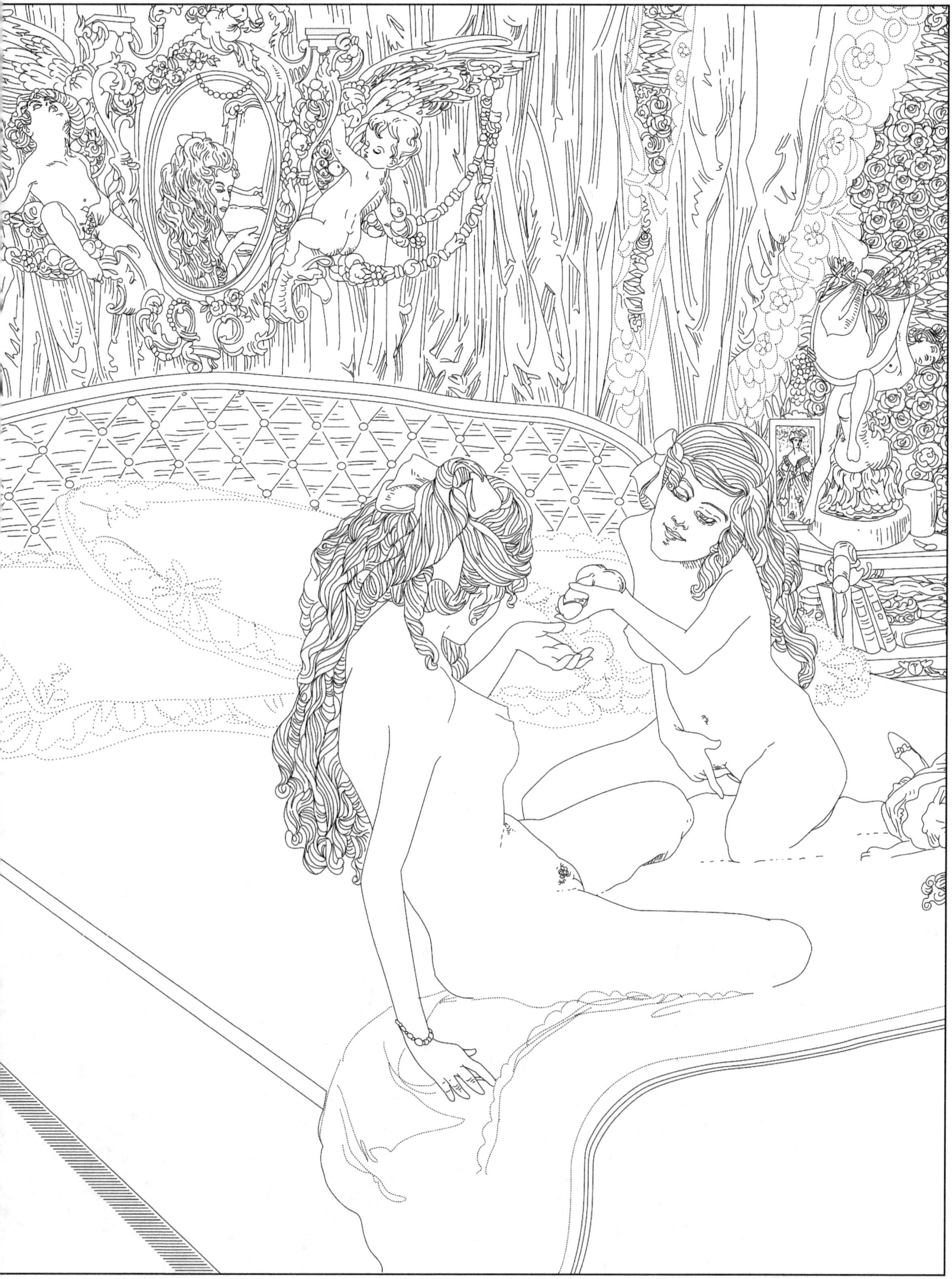

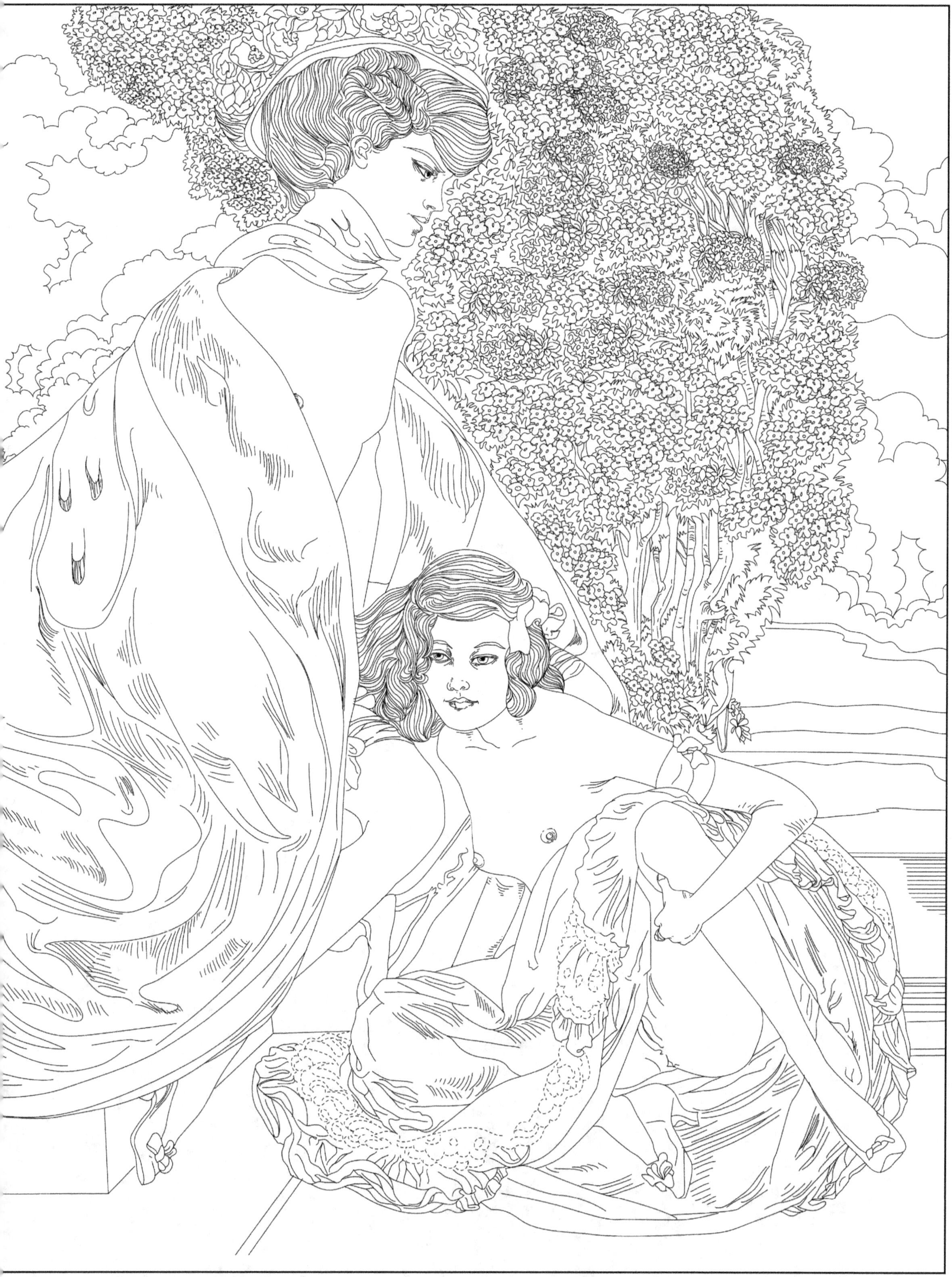

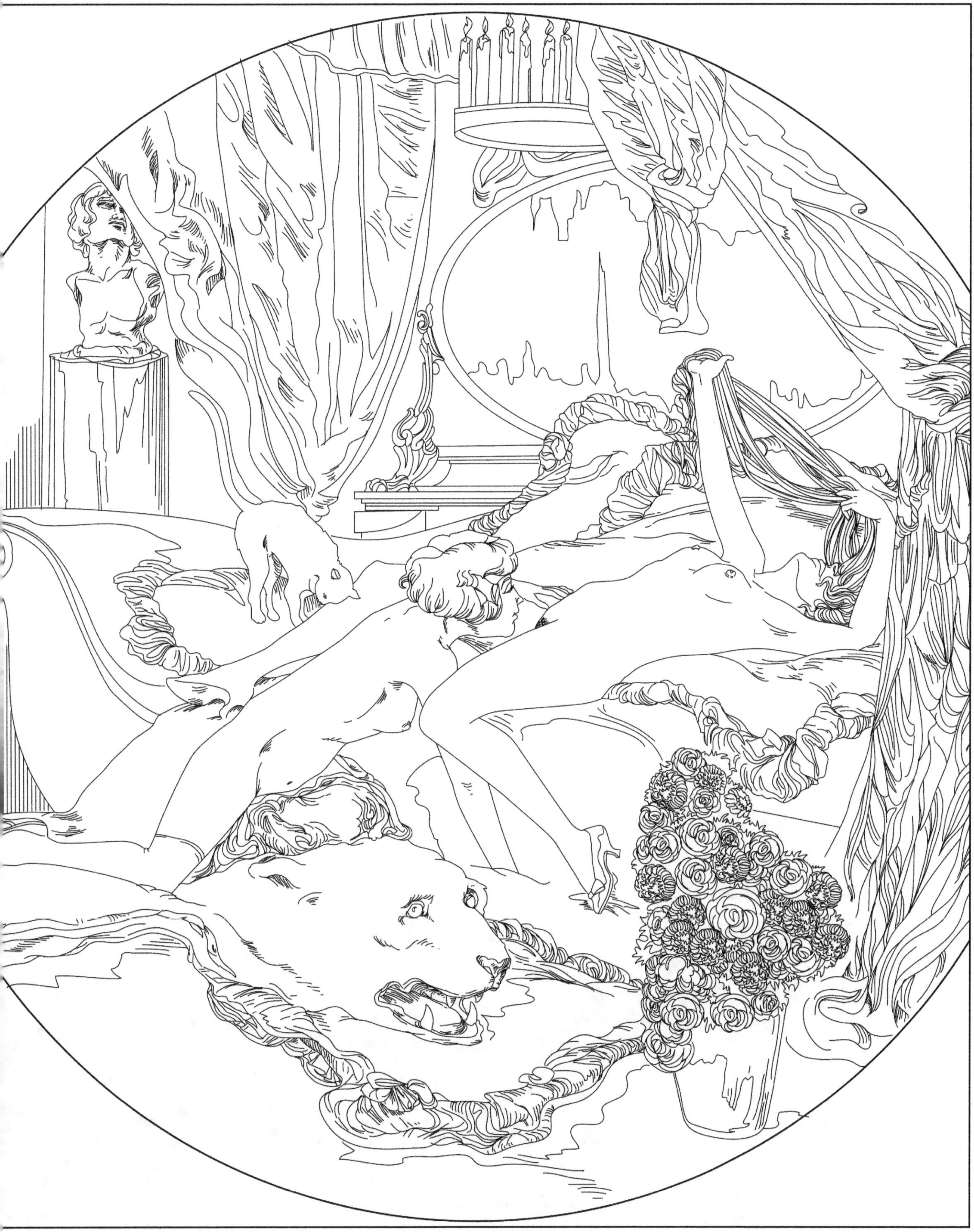

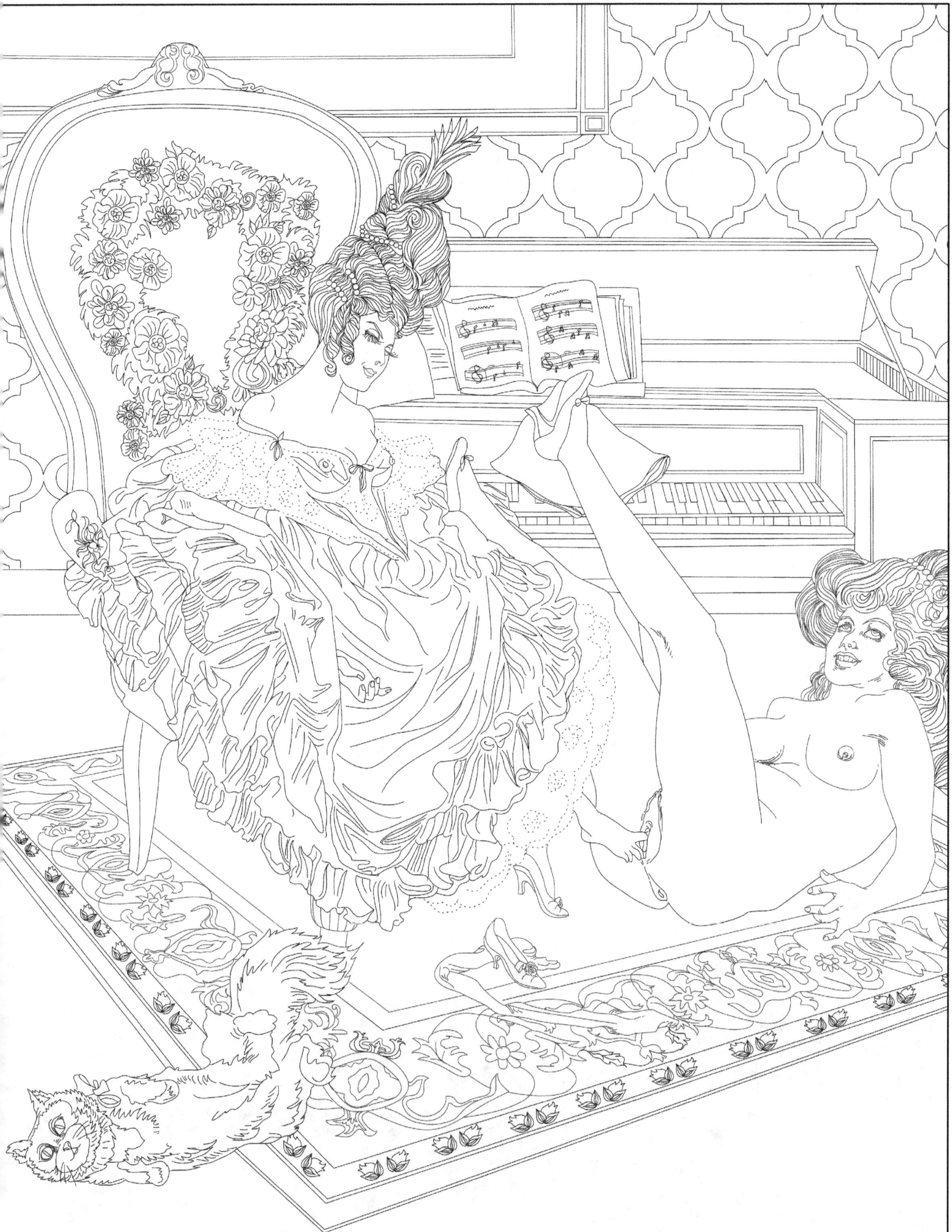

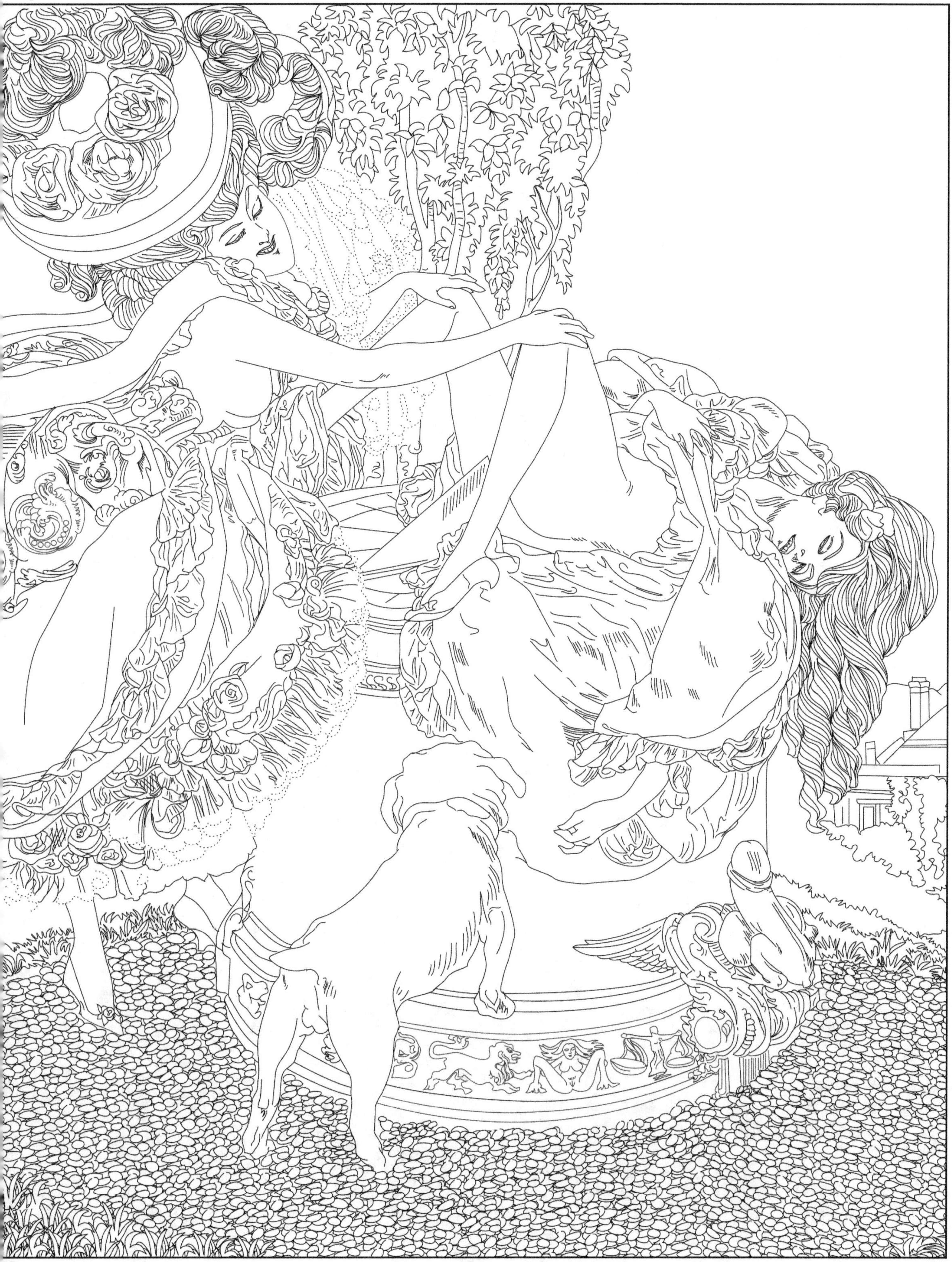

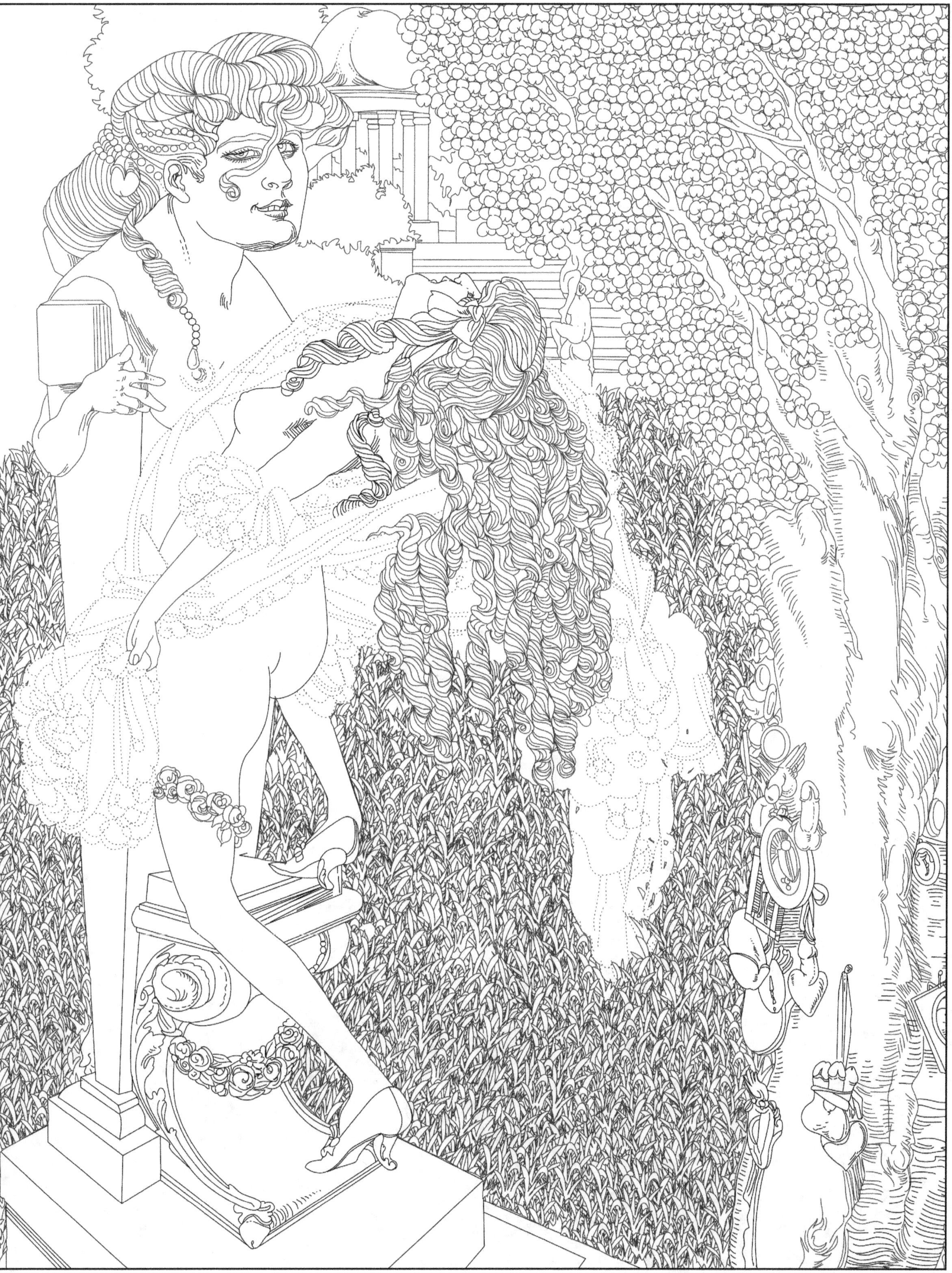

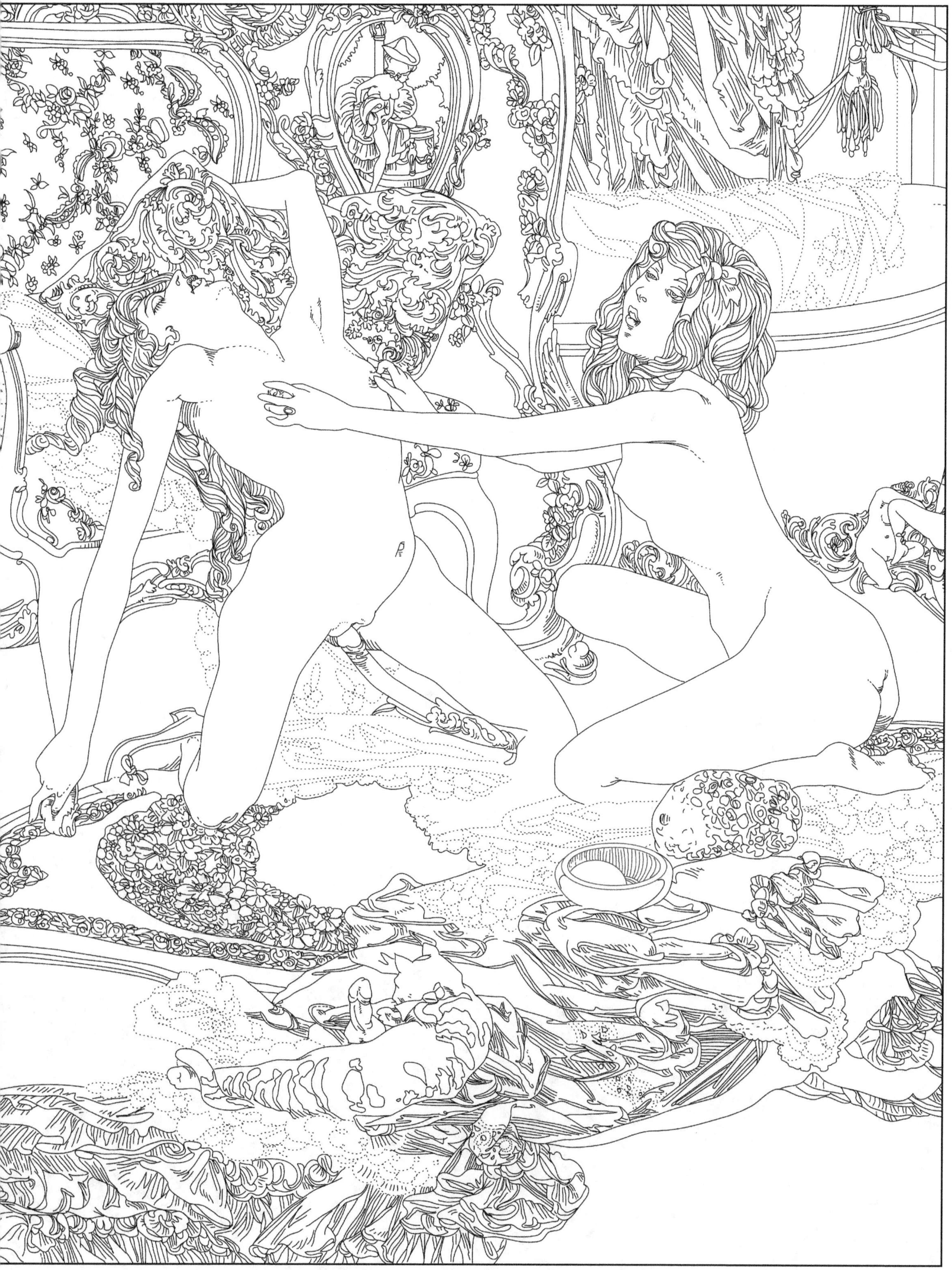

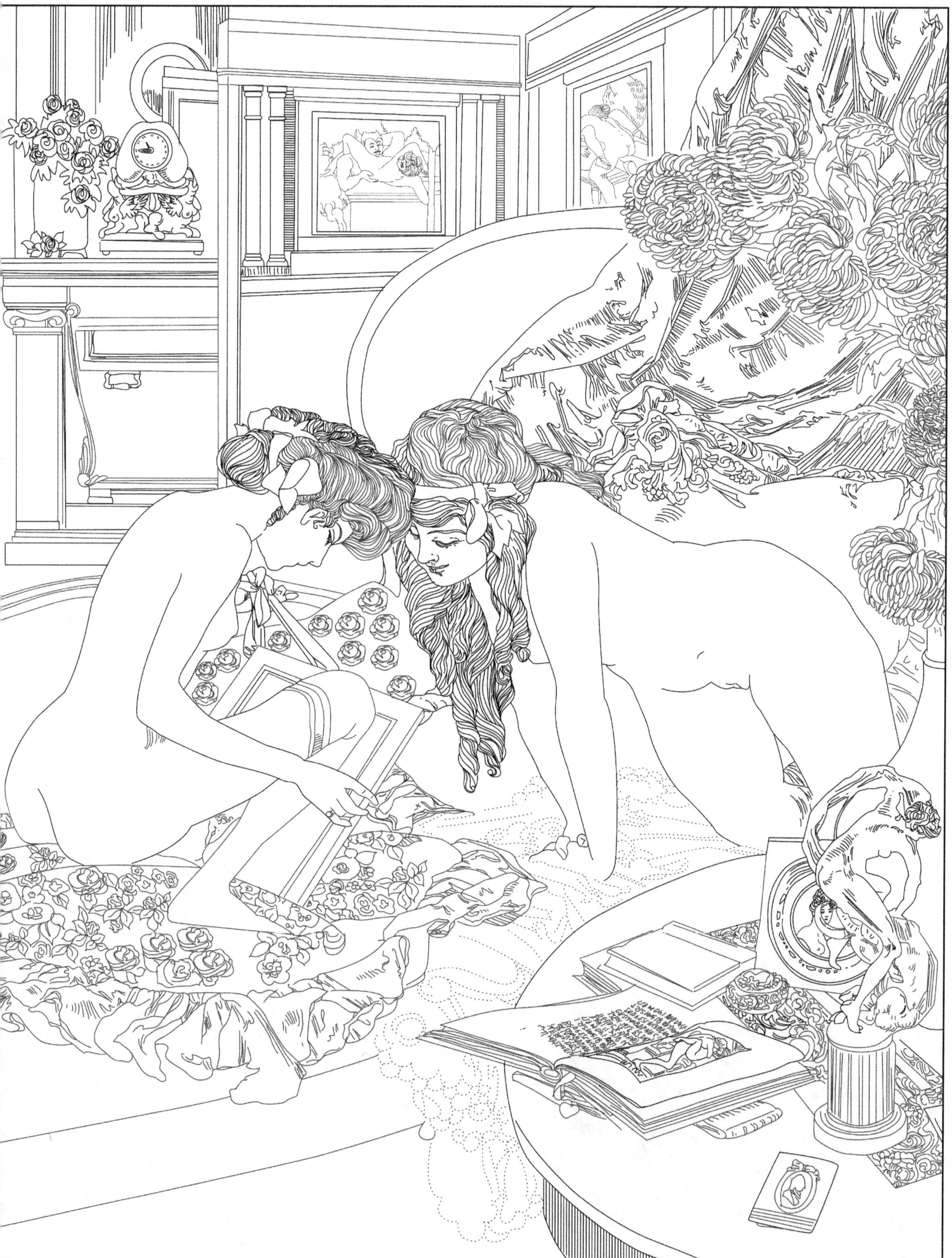

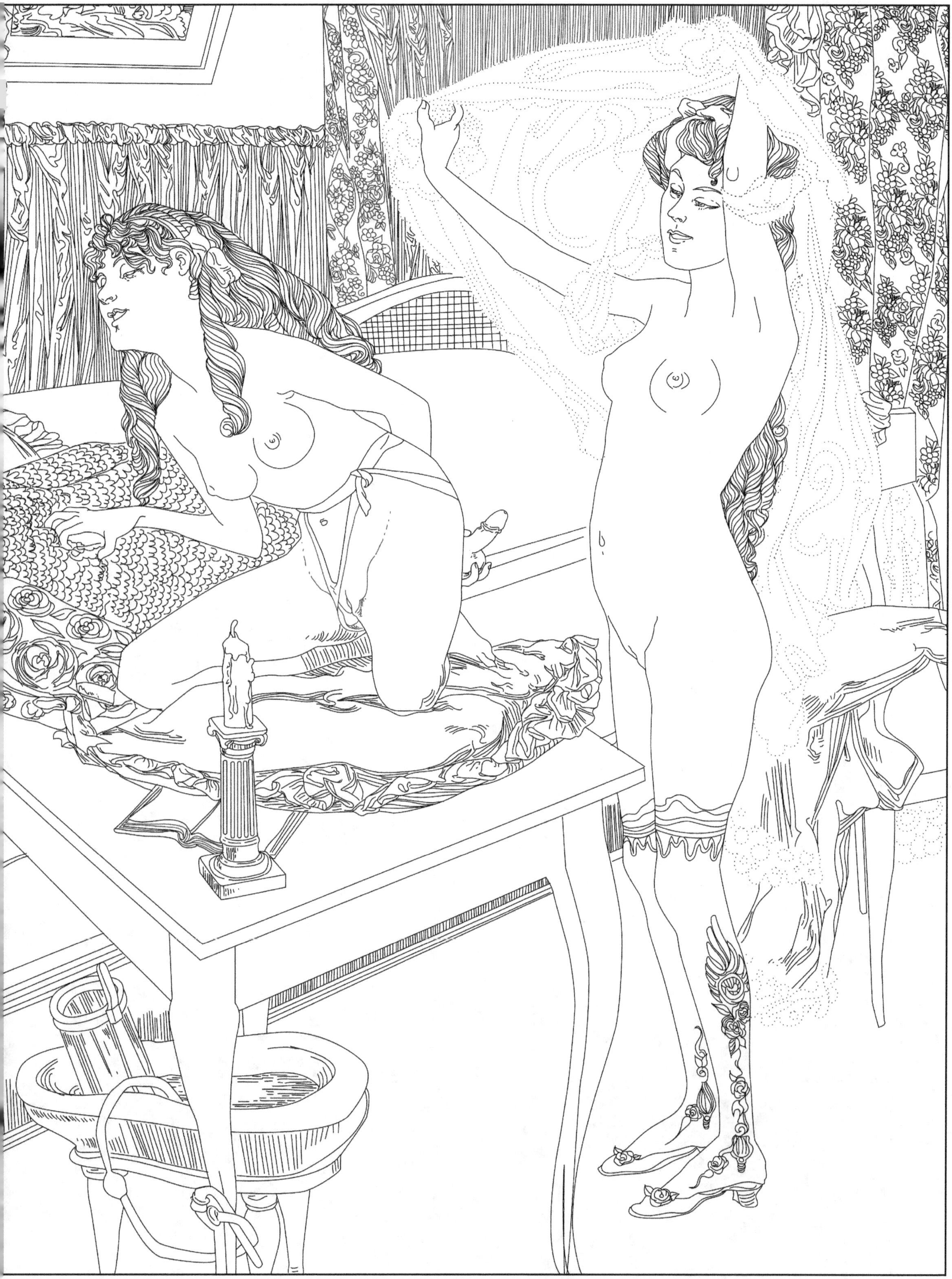

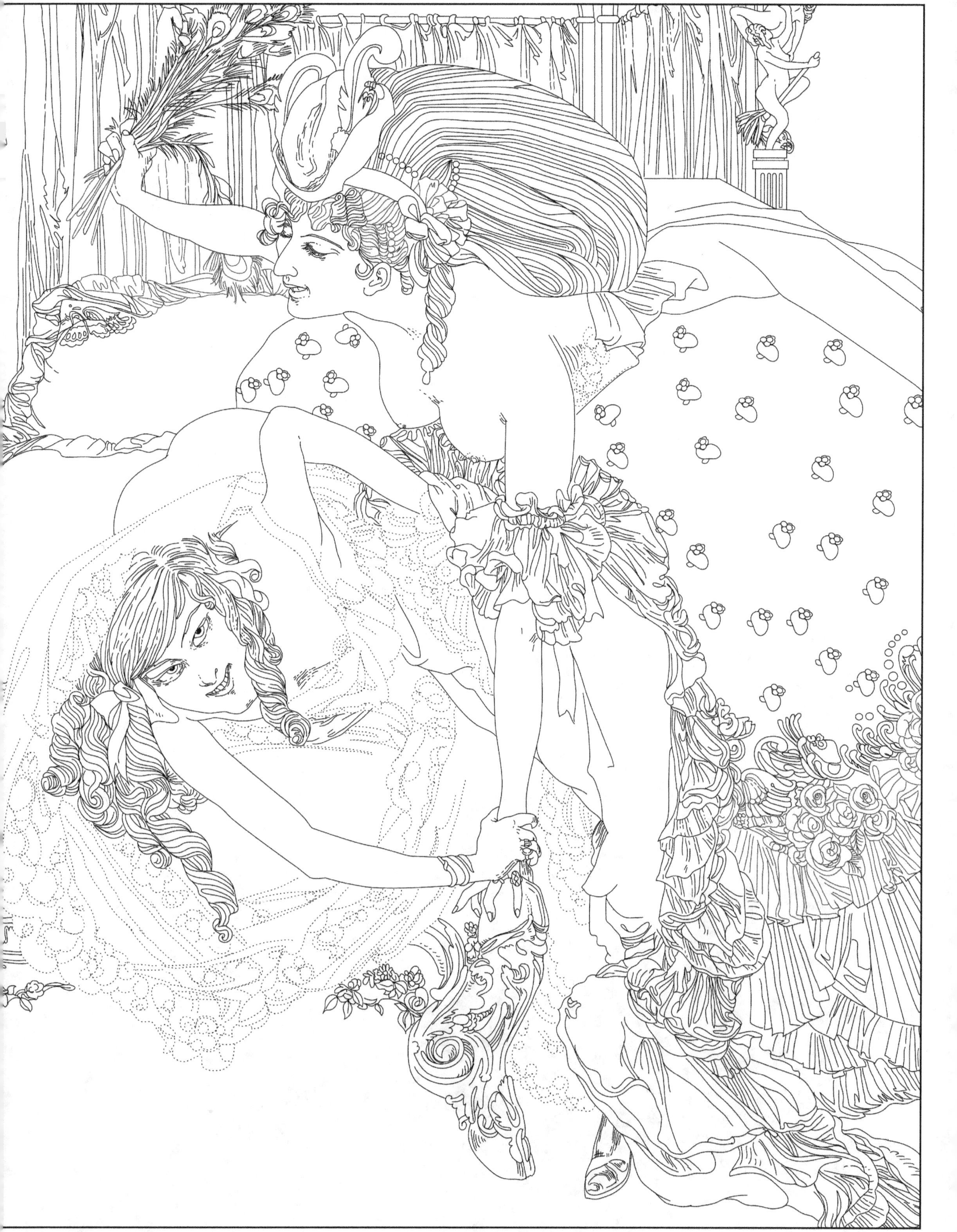

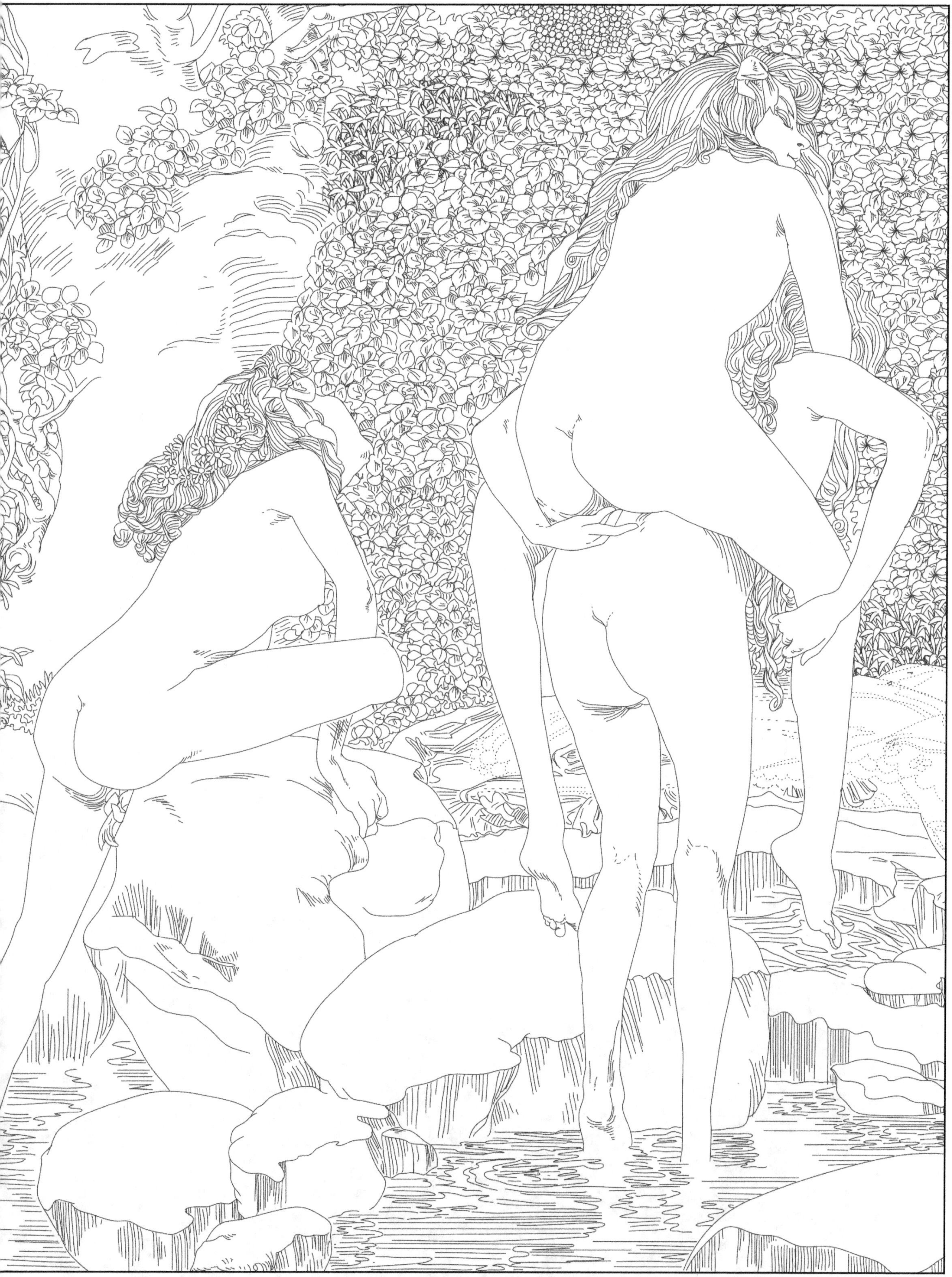

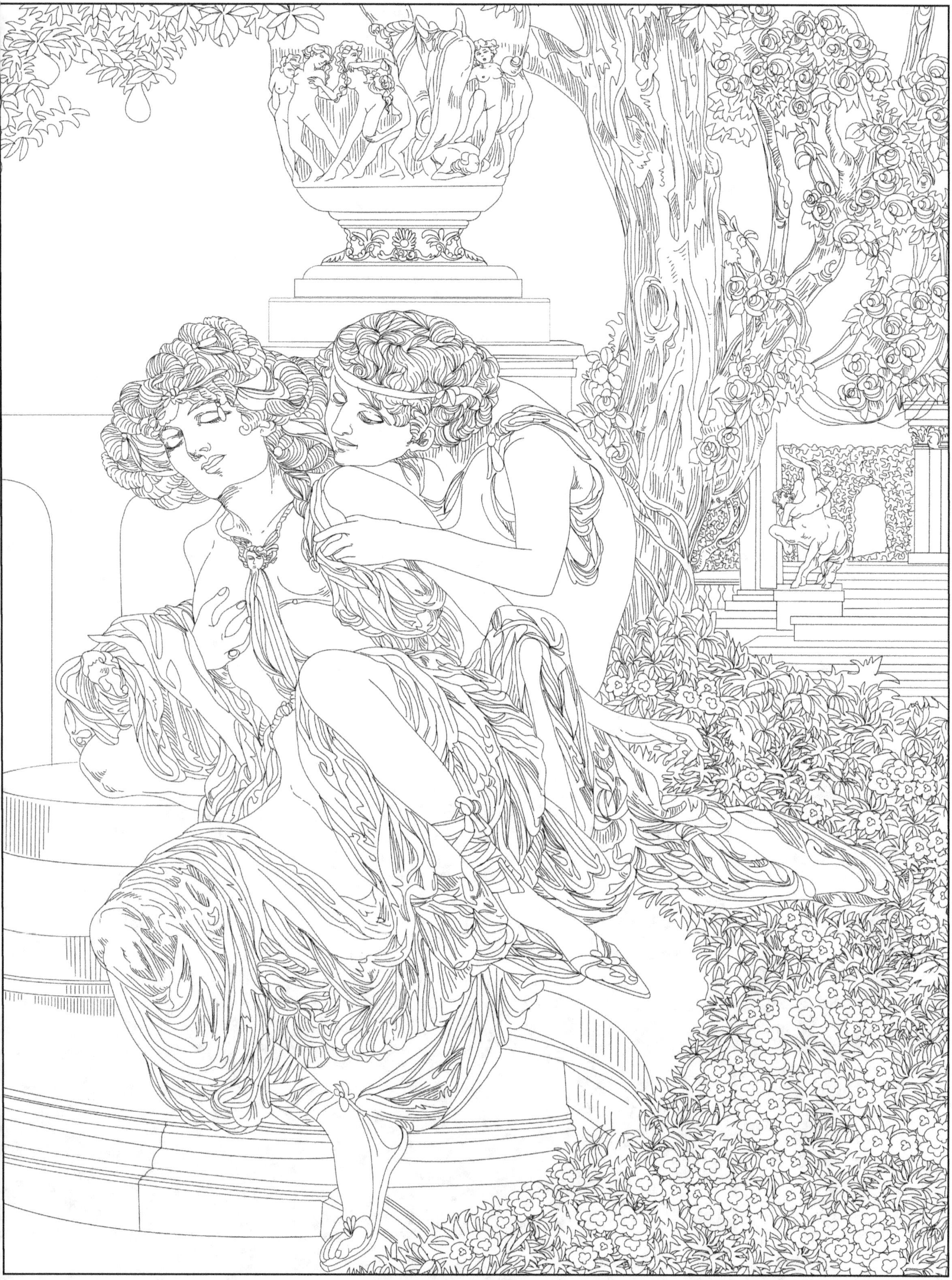

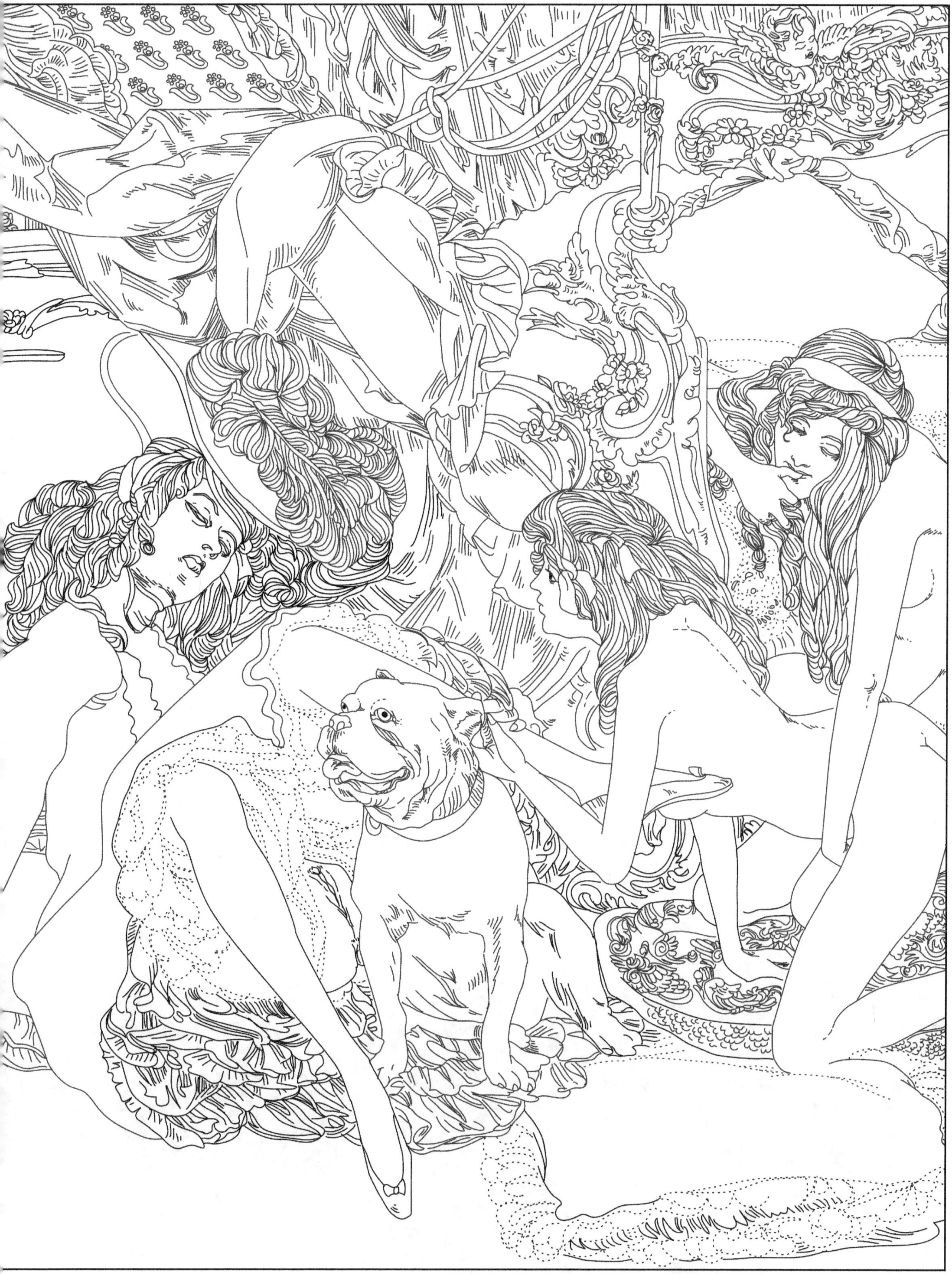

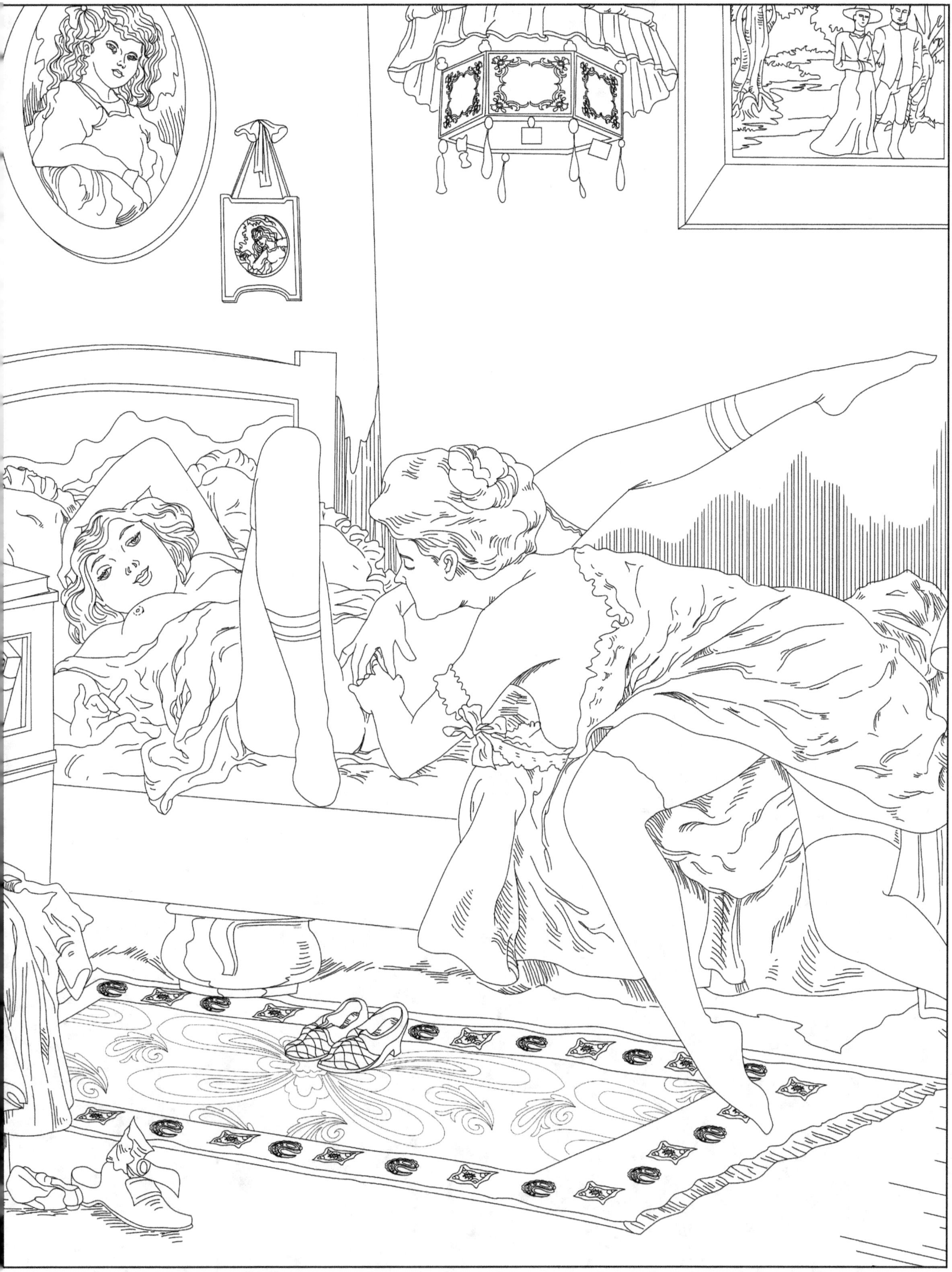

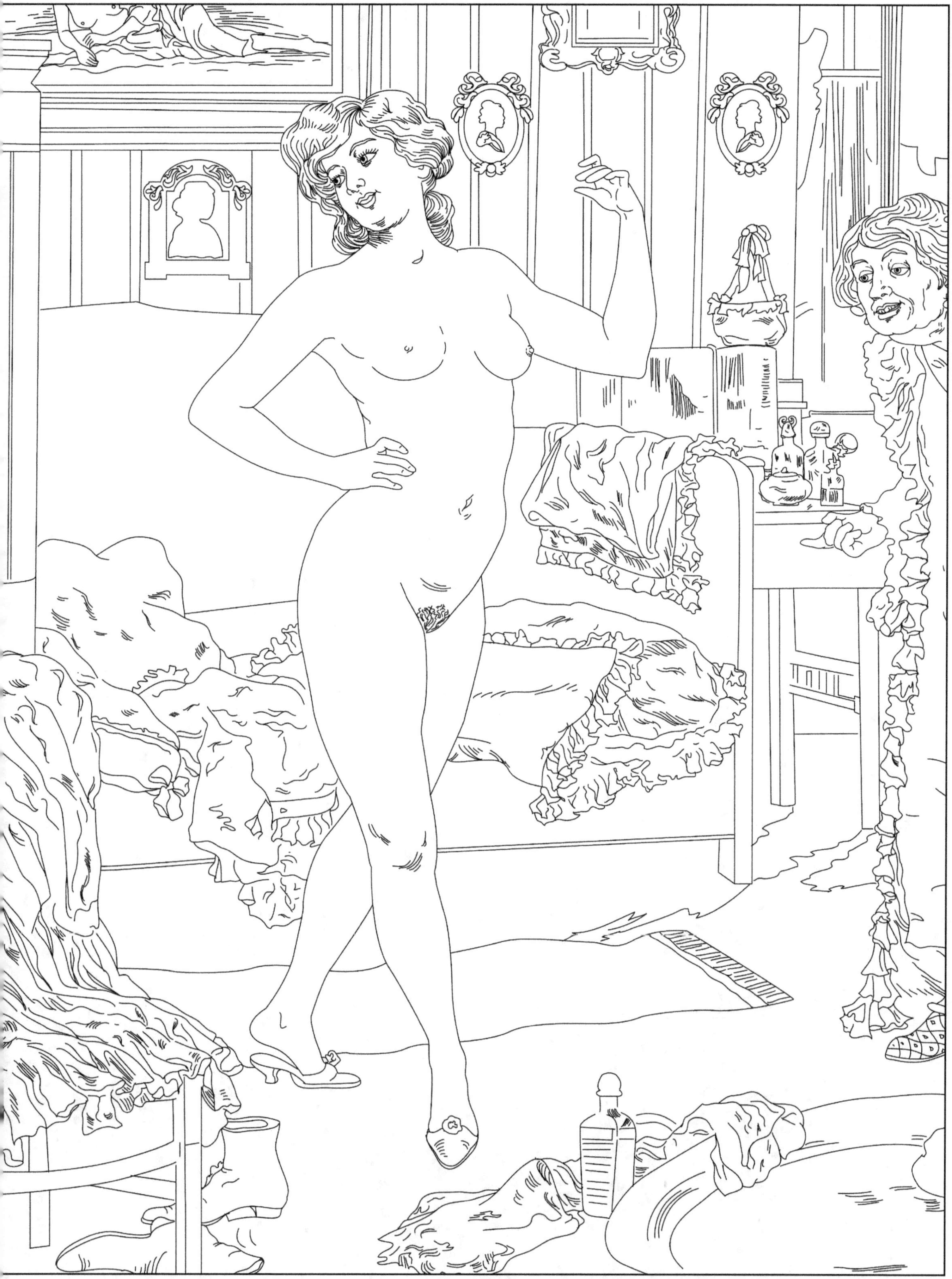

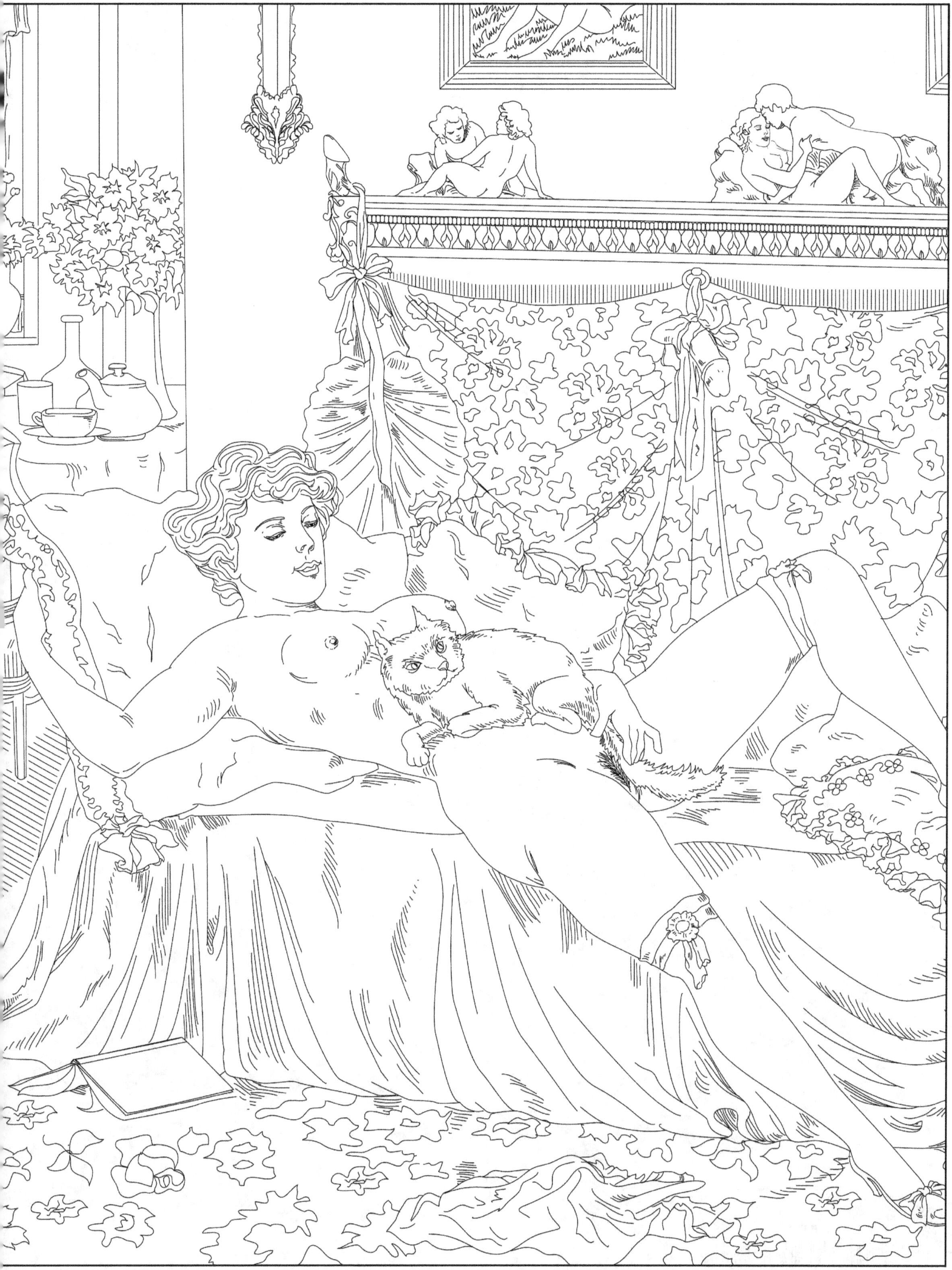

www.ingramcontent.com/pod-product-compliance
Lightning Source LLC
Chambersburg PA
CBHW081622220526
45468CB00010B/2984
* 9 7 8 1 8 8 7 5 9 3 6 2 5 *